First World War
and Army of Occupation
War Diary
France, Belgium and Germany

35 DIVISION
105 Infantry Brigade,
Brigade Machine Gun Company
11 May 1916 - 31 January 1918

WO95/2488/4

The Naval & Military Press Ltd
www.nmarchive.com
Published in association with The National Archives

Published by

The Naval & Military Press Ltd

Unit 10 Ridgewood Industrial Park,

Uckfield, East Sussex,

TN22 5QE England

Tel: +44 (0) 1825 749494

www.naval-military-press.com

www.nmarchive.com

This diary has been reprinted in facsimile from the original. Any imperfections are inevitably reproduced and the quality may fall short of modern type and cartographic standards.

© **Crown Copyright**
Images reproduced by permission of The National Archives, London, England, 2015.

Contents

Document type	Place/Title	Date From	Date To
Heading	35th Division 105th Infy Bde 105th Machine Gun Coy. May 1916-Jan 1918.		
War Diary		11/05/1916	27/05/1916
War Diary		26/05/1916	30/06/1916
Miscellaneous	D.A.G. 3rd Echelon.		
Heading	105th Bde. 35th Div. War Diary 105th Brigade Machine Gun Company 1st to 31st July 1916.		
War Diary	Belzage Farm.	01/07/1916	03/07/1916
War Diary	Lucheux	04/07/1916	07/07/1916
War Diary	Beauval.	08/07/1916	14/07/1916
War Diary	Billonwood.	15/07/1916	16/07/1916
War Diary	Bernafay & Trones Wds.	17/07/1916	21/07/1916
War Diary	Billon Wood.	22/07/1916	23/07/1916
War Diary	Carnoy.	24/07/1916	25/07/1916
War Diary	Briqueterie.	26/07/1916	31/07/1916
War Diary	Sandpit Valley.	31/03/1918	31/03/1918
Miscellaneous		01/07/1916	31/07/1916
Heading	105th Brigade. 35th Division. 105th Brigade Machine Gun Company August 1916.		
War Diary		01/08/1916	31/08/1916
War Diary		01/08/1916	30/09/1916
War Diary	In the Field.	01/09/1916	30/09/1916
War Diary	Arras.	01/10/1916	31/10/1916
Miscellaneous	Original.		
War Diary	In the Field.	01/11/1916	31/12/1916
War Diary	In the Field.	01/01/1917	31/01/1917
War Diary	Houvin-Houvigneul.	01/02/1917	08/02/1917
War Diary	Fremont.	09/02/1917	18/02/1917
War Diary	De Muin.	19/02/1917	28/02/1917
War Diary	Chilly Sector.	01/03/1917	23/03/1917
War Diary	Hyencourt Le Petit.	24/03/1917	01/04/1917
War Diary	Mesnil Le Petit.	02/04/1917	03/04/1917
War Diary	Hombleux.	04/04/1917	12/04/1917
War Diary	Merancourt.	13/04/1917	13/04/1917
War Diary	Villeveque.	14/04/1917	10/05/1917
War Diary	Marteville.	11/05/1917	19/05/1917
War Diary	Trefcon.	20/05/1917	23/05/1917
War Diary	Peronne.	24/05/1917	25/05/1917
War Diary	Sorel Le Grand.	26/05/1917	26/05/1917
War Diary	Aizecourt Le Bas.	27/05/1917	01/06/1917
War Diary	Villers.	02/06/1917	07/06/1917
War Diary	Cuislain.	08/06/1917	17/06/1917
War Diary	Aizecourt Le Bas.	17/06/1917	24/06/1917
War Diary	Gauchewood.	25/06/1917	01/07/1917
War Diary	Villers Faucon.	02/07/1917	06/07/1917
War Diary	Ephey.	07/07/1917	13/07/1917
War Diary	Aizecourt Le Bas.	14/07/1917	22/07/1917
War Diary	St Emilie.	23/07/1917	31/07/1917
War Diary	St Emilie.	01/09/1917	02/09/1917
War Diary	Aizecourt-Le-Bas.	03/09/1917	17/09/1917

War Diary	Lempire.	18/09/1917	31/09/1917
War Diary	Lempire Road.	01/09/1917	09/09/1917
War Diary	St. Emilie.	10/09/1917	13/09/1917
War Diary	Aizecourt-Le-Bas.	13/09/1917	18/09/1917
War Diary	Parrs Bank Nr Epeny.	19/09/1917	01/10/1917
Heading	War Diary Of No. 105 M.G. Coy. for October, 1917. Vol 18.		
War Diary	Peronne.	01/10/1917	04/10/1917
War Diary	Dainville.	04/10/1917	11/10/1917
War Diary	Arras.	11/10/1917	11/10/1917
War Diary	Leuringhem.	12/10/1917	14/10/1917
War Diary	Proven.	15/10/1917	16/10/1917
War Diary	Flverdinghe.	16/10/1917	23/10/1917
War Diary	Bosinghe.	23/10/1917	31/10/1917
War Diary	J. Camp Near Woeten.	01/11/1917	05/11/1917
War Diary	Plaistowe Camp Near Proven.	06/11/1917	15/11/1917
War Diary	Browne Camp Nr Poperinghe.	16/11/1917	24/11/1917
War Diary	Kempton Park.	25/11/1917	29/11/1917
War Diary	Siege Camp.	30/11/1917	08/12/1917
War Diary	Le Nouveau Monde.	09/12/1917	10/12/1917
War Diary	Poperinghe.	11/12/1917	31/12/1917
War Diary	School Camp.	01/01/1918	09/01/1918
War Diary	Solferino Camp.	10/01/1918	17/01/1918
War Diary	Kempton Park.	18/01/1918	23/01/1918
War Diary	Canal Bank.	24/01/1918	31/01/1918
Heading	15 Notts & Derby Vol 2.		

35TH DIVISION
105TH INFY BDE

105TH MACHINE GUN COY.
MAY 1916-JAN 1918

War diary of
105th Brigade Machine Gun Company

May 11th 1916 — Company entrained at the military siding GRANTHAM at 3.30am, detrained at SOUTHAMPTON about 2pm, embarked on board H.M. Hired Transport CITY OF DUNKIRK

May 12th — reached LE HAVRE about 3am the next day. Company disembarked about 8am & marched to No 2 rest camp.

May 13th — Stores etc drawn from ordnance, and entrained at Point 6 GARE MARITIME about 10pm.

May 14th — Reached ROUEN about 6am, where we had a 12 hours halt. Men detrained, animals & limbers left on their trucks. Moved off again at about 6pm.

May 15th — Detrained about 11am at LESTREM near MERVILLE and marched to huts, near 105th Brigade Headquarters 1 mile North of VEILLE CHAPELLE.

May 16th to May 20th — Officers looked round & studied the Brigade front about NEUVE CHAPELLE. During this period also, each section went up for 24 hours instruction without guns, being attached to the Lewis gun sections of Battalions.

May 21st — Company took up its position in the line
No 1 Section 4 battle emplacements in the front line.
No 4 Section 2 battle emplacements in the front line & two guns Chateau East & Chateau South
No 2 Section 2 guns PORT ARTHUR post and 2 guns OXFORD keep
No 3 Section 2 guns PONT LOGY NORTH 1 gun PONT LOGY South

original

War diary of 105 Bde Machine Gun Coy.
(continued)

May 21st (cont) — and one gun at LANDSDOWNE. Company Headquarters were situated at EUSTON CORNER, ¾ mile East of ROUGE CROIX on the ESTAIRES – LA BASSÉE Rd. The Company paraded at 4 am, marched to the rendez-vous where guides & a carrying party provided by the Infantry met us. The relief began about 4.45 am. The relief was accomplished without any difficulty some of the parties however being shelled slightly as they went in. There were no casualties.
There were in all 6 Vickers and 4 Lewis guns in the front line in Battle Emplacements and 7 mobile Lewis guns.
PONT LOGY NORTH, PONT LOGY SOUTH OXFORD and PORT ARTHUR were all shelled to-day. No casualties.

May 22nd — at 0.30 am a hostile working party was fired on by 1 gun of No 1 Section in conjunction with the Battalion Lewis guns. Traversing & Vertical Searching was afterwards carried out in the hope of finding enemy carrying parties. No of rounds fired 750. The gun fired well but there were a considerable number of NO 3 Jams caused by badly filled belts. These belts were all carefully checked before going up & must have been caused by jolting whilst carrying.

May 23rd — about 2.30 am two enemy wiring parties were fired on & dispersed. The gun worked well & there were no stoppages. About 3 pm two guns opened indirect fire from the neighbourhood of PONT LOGY, in co-operation with the Artillery who were firing on a portion of the fire trench. Our target was a communication trench leading back from this

Original

War diary of 105th Brigade Machine Gun Coy
(Continued)

May 23rd (cont) portion. One gun which was in the open was shelled by shrapnel & had to cease fire after having fired about 60 rounds. The other gun fired about 500 rounds, using diagonal traversing.

At 10.10 pm one gun near the same place opened fire, using vertical searching, from the cross roads at LA TOURELLE to the DISTILLERY. Range 2600 to 2800. One belt was fired.

Night May 23/24th During this night one gun in the front line in conjunction with battalion Lewis guns kept up a fire on the gaps made in the enemy's wire & parapet during the previous afternoon. This gun fired 17 belts & in the morning it was found that the enemy had done very little repairing work.

Night 24th/25th Gaps in enemy's wire continually fired on by guns in the front line. Indirect fire was used on the communication trench fired at on the afternoon of 23rd May.

May 25th Morning quiet. In the afternoon indirect fire used as yesterday.

Night 25/26th Gaps in enemy's wire & parapet continually fired at.

May 26th Morning & afternoon quiet with the exception of a few whizz bangs near No 9 Battle Emplacement. Our first casualty Pte Walton No 4 Section being slightly wounded.

Night 26th/27th From Stand to till about 10.30 pm one gun fired at gaps made in the enemy's parapet two days ago. From 11 pm till about 2 am, 3 Vickers guns fired indirect, 2 guns using traversing &

original

War diary of 105 Machine Gun Coy
(Continued)

Night 26/27th May (cont)

vertical searching on the BOIS DE BIEZ & one gun searching the neighbourhood of LA RUSSE, where a hostile battery had been located.

During the night before, a dummy emplacement had been built in the open ground between PONT LOGY NORTH & CHIMNEY CRESCENT in the old German Trenches, while indirect fire was being used, this emplacement was shelled by about 15 or 16 heavy Shrapnell. It would appear therefore that the ruse succeeded. The emplacement was made of new sand bags & a large loophole facing the enemy.

May 27th

Inter section reliefs took place without incident
No 1 Section going to OXFORD & PORT ARTHUR
No 2 " " to 4 Battle emplacements front line
No 3 " " to CHATEAU & 2 in front line
No 4 " " PONT LOGY NORTH & SOUTH & LANDSDOWNE.

During the night 27th/28th the cross roads at LA TOURELLE & the DISTILLERY were fired at from the neighbourhood of PONT LOGY. Front line guns fired at gaps in enemy's wire & parapet, in conjunction with Battalion Lewis guns.

May 28th

Morning & afternoon quiet, during the night 28/29th 4 guns in co-operation with the artillery ~~thoroughly~~ thoroughly searched the BOIS DE BIEZ & LA RUSSE 8,000 rounds were fired.

May 29th

Morning & afternoon quiet. during the night 29th/30th in co-operation with artillery who were covering a raiding party, 6 guns fired indirect from near PONT LOGY on the BOIS de BIEZ, LA RUSSE & LES BRULOT, rain was falling all

original

105 Machine Gun Company
War Diary of

Night 29/30th May (cont) — the time. One casualty to-day Pte McCallum 15th Cheshire Regt- attached to the company.

May 30th — Morning & afternoon quiet. About 7.30 pm the enemy started to violently bombard our front line trenches - back line posts & keeps till about 10.30 pm. A raiding party entered the trenches but did not remain long. Unfortunately no Vickers gun was near enough the point of entry to see them, there being a mist greatly augmented by shell smoke. Casualties to the company were heavy, 2/Lts Canning, Abbotts & Graham being wounded, the first & last seriously, the other slightly. Pte Bisk No 2 Section killed early next morning by a sniper & Ptes Whamby & Callaghan wounded.

After the bombardment 4 guns fired from 12 midnight 30th/31st on the enemy's parapet & BOIS DE BIEZ. No guns or emplacements were damaged, all telephone communication with the front line was broken almost immediately, but the line to the Brigade held out until about 9.30 pm.

May 31st — Morning afternoon & night quiet up till 12 noon. During the afternoon delivered fire was used into the BOIS DE BIEZ. 2/Lt Russell Jones brought up help as we were very short of officers, 2/Lt Jenkins having gone sick the afternoon before. The company has now been in the trenches & keeps continuously since the 21st May.

original

105 Machine Gun Company
War diary of

May 31st — our total casualties being
one man killed
3 officers + 4 men wounded
1 officer & 1 man sick (Pte Clarkson)
Soon after getting into the trenches, each
regiment in the Brigade sent 4 men to be
attached to the company.

A S Jordan Major
105 Machine Gun Company

12 mn 31/5/16.

105th Brigade Machine Gun Company
War diary
June 1916

June 1st — Quiet day & night.
During the evening two guns fired indirect on the BOIS DE BIEZ. During the night one gun fired on the enemy's parapet & wire.

June 2nd — Morning & afternoon quiet.
During the night two guns fired indirect on the BOIS DE BIEZ. The S.E. corner, where a gun position has been located, was especially searched.

June 3rd — Morning & afternoon quiet.
During the night one gun fired from 9-30 pm to midnight on S.E. corner of BOIS DE BIEZ. Another at same target from a different position from midnight to 2 am. The enemy shelled back without getting anywhere near us.

June 4th — Morning & afternoon quiet.
Enemy appeared to be searching for our indirect fire positions with shrapnel.
No indirect fire was done at night owing to a strong wind. Our front line guns played on the enemy's parapet & wire.

June 5th — A few enemy trench mortars came over about 100x in rear of our No. 1 battle emplacement in the front line. No damage.
During the night indirect fire used against the BOIS DE BIEZ.

II.   105th Brigade Machine Gun Coy.

June 1916.   War Diary

June 6th Morning & afternoon quiet.
Indirect fire used from 11 p.m. to 11-45 p.m. on the DISTILLERY.
11-45 to 12-30 on the S.E. corner of BOIS DE BIEZ.
A German M.G. fired overhead during the night along the LA BASSEE road. Our M.G. using traversing & vertical searching silenced him after two bursts.

June 7th Quiet day & night.
A few enemy 5-9 H.E. came over near our No.6. front line gun position breaching the parapet.
No indirect fire at night : new positions being prepared.

June 8th Morning & afternoon quiet.
During the operations which took place at 9 p.m. 6 Vickers guns fired indirect of the following targets
(1) LaRUSSE (enemy battery)
(2) FERME du BIEZ
(3) LA TOURELLE
(4) DISTILLERY
(5) S.E. corner of Bois de BIEZ (battery)
(6) BOIS de BIEZ
(7) Tramways, paths etc. behind the Bois

14,000 rounds were fired during the bombardment.
Three Vickers in conjunction with battalion Lewis guns swept enemy's parapet & searched the re-entrant.   After the operations

III   105th Brigade Machine Gun Company
             War Diary

             June 1916

8th (contd.) very little indirect fire could be used owing to the wet & muddy condition of the guns & belts. Front line Vickers continued to fire at the breaches & further back during the remainder of the night.

June 9th Morning & afternoon quiet.
During the night indirect was used on the BOIS DE BIEZ & paths behind. In the front line our Vickers guns fired from the parapet at enemy front line & machine guns.

June 10th Quiet day & night.
Our Vickers guns fired indirect during the night on the BOIS DE BIEZ & paths behind.
The Vickers in the front line played on the enemy's parapet & barbed wire. One gun dispersed an enemy working party opposite the NEB at 10.30 pm & continued traversing on this spot, preventing any further attempts at work on the part of the Huns.

June 11th Quiet day & night.
Vickers guns fired from the parapet during the night & indirect was used on the LA TOURELLE & the DISTILLERY.

June 12th Day & night quiet. Our Vickers fired indirect at the usual targets during the night.

June 13th Day & night quiet. Weather very wet. Indirect fire used by our Vickers during the night.

[IV]

105th Brigade Machine Gun Company
War Diary   June 1916

June 14th — Quiet day & night. Our Vickers fired indirect on the usual targets during the night.

June 15 — Quiet day & night. Our Vickers fired indirect at N.E. corner of BOIS DE BIEZ. Our front line guns used the same target.

June 16th — Quiet day & night. Our Vickers fired indirect at usual targets during the night. The 105th Brigade goes out today & tomorrow, but we have been attached to the 183rd Brigade for the present.

June 17 — Day quiet. The gas alarm sounded at 12-45 p.m. Everyone 'stood to' with gas helmets & the guns of the section that are resting were ready for firing. No gas was smelt & at 2-15 a.m. we stood down. During all this time we were unable to get into telephonic communication with Brigade Headquarters.

June 18 — Quiet day & night. Our Vickers employed the usual indirect fire at night.

June 19 — At 2-15 a.m. our Artillery & T.M. bombarded the crater at M.36.1.½ our Vickers in No.20 emplacement was used from the parapet.

June 20 — Quiet day. At 10-30 p.m. our Artillery & T.M.s bombarded the enemy for 10 minutes. We had not been informed that anything was to take place so could not participate in the scheme & do not know what was intended.

105th Brigade Machine Gun Coy.

V

June 1916   War Diary

June 21   Quiet day. Three of our Vickers fired indirect during the night. The 182nd Brigade relieved the 183rd during the day & night. We have been transferred to the former pending the arrival & instruction of the 182nd M.G. Coy.

June 22   Quiet day. At 12-5 a.m. a strombos horn was heard some distance away, direction uncertain. The matter was reported to Brigade H.Q. No gas was smelt.

June 23   Quiet day & night. Our Vickers in the front line fired on enemy's wire etc. as usual.

June 24   The 183rd Machine Gun Coy. came up for instruction.

June 25   Quiet day. At 11-15 p.m. 8 of our guns together with others of 182nd, 183rd & 104th Coys. 48 in all, fired one belt, sweeping the ground between LA TOURELLE & AUBERS. At 11-15 p.m. our remaining 8 guns in front line with the 8 of other Coys played on the enemy's parapet. Another belt was fired by all guns at 11-45 p.m. The Right group of Artillery gave support, firing from 11-15 to 11-30 p.m. & 11-45 to 11-55 p.m.

VI   War diary

June 1916.

June 27. The gaps in the enemy's wire were kept open during the day. The enemy retaliated on our front line. At 11-40 p.m. The Artillery bombarded the enemy for 20 minutes & a party of Warwicks made a raid. The company was due for relief on the night 27/28 but left one gun in the front line

28th & 4 guns at PONT LOGY to cooperate; the latter with indirect fire. The company had now been in the line for 37 days.
The Company went into rest billets at BALZAGE FARM, rejoining the 105th Brigade.

June 29 & 30. The Company cleaned the guns & themselves & got ready generally for the next move. Spare are exceedingly difficult to obtain & we are very short of several parts rendered useless by the long spell of work.

105th Bde.
35th Div.

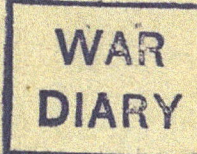

105th BRIGADE

MACHINE GUN COMPANY

1st to 31st JULY 1916.

WAR DIARY or INTELLIGENCE SUMMARY

105th M.G. Coy   Vol 3

(Erase heading not required.)

Place	Date 1916	Hour	Summary of Events and Information	Remarks and references to Appendices
BELZAGE FARM.	July 1		Company Training.	
"	2		"	
"	3		The company marched to CHOQUES where it detrained & proceeded to BOUQUEMAISON, then it detrained & marched to LUCHEUX.	
LUCHEUX	4		Cleaning guns etc.	
"	5		Training.	
"	6		"	
"	7		Moved by road to BEAUVAL.	
BEAUVAL	8.		Clean guns & ordnance Training	
"	9		Church Parade	
"	10		Moved by road to BUS-LES-ARTOIS.	
"	11		" " " " WARLOY.	
"	12		" " " " HEILLY.	
"	13		" " " " BOIS CELESTIN.	
"	14		" " " " GROVETOWN thence to BILLON WOOD.	
BILLON WOOD	15		Cleaning do.	
"	16		Section officers reconnoitred BERNAFAY & TRONES WOODS. Coy marched into bivouac to rear of BERNAFAY WOOD.	
BERNAFAY & TRONES WDS.	17.		No 3 Section took up position in BERNAFAY WOOD, Nos 1,2 & 4 Sections in hole of TRONES WOOD.	
"	18.		Warfare — one Lewis shelled, Several casualties.	

WAR DIARY or INTELLIGENCE SUMMARY

(Erase heading not required.)

Place	Date 1916	Hour	Summary of Events and Information	Remarks and references to Appendices
BERNAFAY & TRONES WOOD	19.		One gun of No 4 Section under Lt Braun was sent up on the right of WATERLOT FARM. The enemy MG. were driven by Lt Braun in front. They were fired on in shrapnel uphill. An enemy attack driven back with several casualties. 3 Schults.	
"	20		Sino unseren fel attacks were made on MALTS HORN FARM. 3 of our guns co-operated. Heavy casualties.	
	21		On the night of the 20-21 Coy was relieved by 104 Coy moved back to BILLON WOOD.	
BILLON WOOD	22		Heavily shelled during the night - Transport suffered severely. Moved to TALUS BOIS.	
	23		Coy moved to camp 600's of CARNOY.	
CARNOY	24		Rest.	
	25		Bivouaks, guns & vehicles damaged over etc.	
BRIQUETERIE	26		Coy relieved 104 Coy. 3 guns of No 4 Section in DUBLIN REDOUBT. No 1 Sect in BRIQUETERIE. No 2 + 3 Section in front-line.	
	27		Trench warfare.	
	28		Shelled by Gas + HE.	
	29		Brigade withdrawn from the line. Relieved by 89 + 90th Brigade. Relief very difficult owing to heavy shelling - HE + gas. No 1 Section remained in the line.	
	30		Coy refitting.	
SANDPIT VALLEY	31		Coy less No 1 Section marched to SANDPIT VALLEY. No 1 Section relieved by 164 Coy rejoined Coy.	

Goldale Lt. M.O.C.
105 M.G. Coy.

105th BRIGADE MACHINE GUN COMPANY.

Appendix.

1916.

July.

1st.	The Company is continuing training in billets.
2nd.	We had orders at 7.30 pm. to send forward an officer & N.C.O. to secure billets.
3rd.	The Company proceeded to CHOQUES & entrained at 8 am but the train did not leave until 1 pm. BOUQUE MAISON was reached at 5 pm. & we marched to LUCHEUX, 5 miles off where the company went into billets.
4th, 5th & 6th.	Company carried on with training.
7th. 8th.	The 105th Brigade moved by road to BEAUVAL and continued training.
10th.	Brigade moved from BEAUVAL to BUS-LES-ARTOIS for one night.
11th.	To WARLOY and on
12th.	To HEILLY.
13th.	To GROVE TOWN where company bivouaced.
14th.	To BILLON WOOD.
16th.	To the rear of BERNAFAY WOOD where the company took over from the 54th. One section BERNAFAY & three sections in TRONES Wood. All sixteen guns in the lines
17th.	The company took up positions in BERNAFAY & TRONES Woods including one gun in WATERLOT farm.
18th.	The line was continuously shelled & we sustained several casualties.
19th.	Was One of our guns was pushed out in the neighbourhood of WATERLOT farm & dispersed some of the enemy who were thought to be massing. The gun also silenced an enemy M.G.

Appendix.

1916.

July.

- **20th.** Three guns participated in two infantry attacks during the day. The Objective was MALTS HORN farm but the attacks were not successful. We suffered & also did the infantry.

- **21st.** The company was relieved & went to TALUS BOISE, were our transport suffered from enemy shelling, during the night.

- **23rd.** Moved back 1000^X & bivouaced.

- **26th.** The Coy. relieved the 104 Coy. 1 section in reserve in DUBLIN REDOUBT. 1 sec. at the BRIQUETERIE & two in the line.

- **27th.** The sections in front were heavily shelled one gun team being knocked out.

- **28th.** The company remained in the line.

- **29th.** On the night of 29/30 three sections were relieved & one section left to garrison the BRIQUETERIE.

- **31st.** The Company ~~moved~~ with the exception of one section, moved back to SANDPIT VALLEY & were joined by that section in the night.

105th Brigade.
35th Division.

105th BRIGADE MACHINE GUN COMPANY

AUGUST 1 9 1 6

Army Form C. 2118.

Vol 4

WAR DIARY
or
INTELLIGENCE SUMMARY

(Erase heading not required.)

105 Machine Gun Coy

Instructions regarding War Diaries and Intelligence Summaries are contained in F. S. Regs., Part II. and the Staff Manual respectively. Title Pages will be prepared in manuscript.

Place	Date	Hour	Summary of Events and Information	Remarks and references to Appendices
	1-8-16		Having been relieved the Company marched to the Bois de TAILLE & rested there for two days.	
	4-8-16		The company marched to DAOURS & bivouacked for the night, proceeding at 6-15am on 5/8 to OISSY, 21 miles. Weather very hot & a great deal of dust.	
	5-8-16			
	6-8-16		We were visited by the officers of the 2nd Cie. MITRAILLEUSES, 22e Bataillon de CHASSEURS ALPIN.	
	7-8-16		The MITRAILLEUSE Coy. visited our camping ground, explained their gun & gave a display of drill etc. Men & officers were entertained by us.	
	9-8-16		Transport moved off by road for the CITADEL via DAOURS.	
	10-8-16		The Company marched to HANGEST, entrained to MERICOURT, & marched from there to the CITADEL.	
	12-8-16		The Officers reconnoitred the line from WATERLOT FARM to ARROW HEAD copse. Our 3 General PINNEY (division alger.) inspected the Coy.	
	13-8-16			
	14-8-16 15		Company training.	
	15-8-16			

Army Form C. 2118.

WAR DIARY
or
INTELLIGENCE SUMMARY
(Erase heading not required.)

105 Machine Gun Coy.

Place	Date	Hour	Summary of Events and Information	Remarks and references to Appendices
	19-8-16		No. 4 Sec. proceeded to the line at 7-30 pm. Taking over from No. 9 Coy. Line from TRONES WOOD - GUILLEMONT road to GUILLEMONT - HARDECOURT road. N. Grs. & 3 sections remained at the CITADEL.	
	20-8-16		At 12-30 pm. No. 2 Sec. was ordered to move up to LANCASTER TRENCH & help the 16' CHESHIRE Regt. in an attack on the strong point in the GUILLEMONT - HARDECOURT road & two guns to cover advance from each flank, & afterwards to move up & consolidate. Our heavy artillery bombarded from 12 noon to 7 pm. 18 pounders were to open from 7 - 9 pm. Unfortunately the bombardment the latter CHESHIRES lost heavily & were unable to carry out the attack.	
	21-8-16		No. 2 Sec. relieved No. 4 - relief complete 9-30 am. Remaining 2 Sec. & N. Grs. moved up to the line.	
	22-8-16		Dispositions - No. 2 sec. in line. No. 3 in LANCASTER TRENCH No. 1&4 in dugouts 150' S. of the BRIQUETERIE on the BRIQUETERIE - MARICOURT Rd. At 9 pm. No. 1 sec. with the 16' SHERWOODS took over a piece of line from the GUILLEMONT - HARDECOURT road to N. end of LONELY TRENCH.	
	23-8-16		During the night 23/24 the company was relieved. Heavy enemy shelling greatly delayed matters. One of our guns came into action covering the relief of the infantry. Company rested & cleaned up.	
24-8-16				

Army Form C. 2118.

105 Machine Gun Coy.

WAR DIARY
or
INTELLIGENCE SUMMARY
(Erase heading not required.)

Instructions regarding War Diaries and Intelligence Summaries are contained in F. S. Regs., Part II. and the Staff Manual respectively. Title Pages will be prepared in manuscript.

Place	Date	Hour	Summary of Events and Information	Remarks and references to Appendices
	26-5-16		Company marched off at 2.30 pm to SAND PIT VALLEY	
	28-5-16		Company marched to BOIS de TAILLE	
	29-5-16		The Transport started at 11 am on a two days march to RIBEAUCOURT, spending the night at COISY.	
	30-5-16		At 1 am the remainder of the company marched to HEILLY & entrained for CANDAS arriving at 12 noon; detrained & marched to RIBEAUCOURT.	
	31-5-16		Company marched off at 9-15 am for LUCHEUX arriving at 6-30 pm.	

2449 Wt. W14957/M90 750,000 1/16 J.B.C. & A. Forms/C.2118/12.

WAR DIARY
or
INTELLIGENCE SUMMARY

(Erase heading not required.)

Army Form C. 2118.

Instructions regarding War Diaries and Intelligence Summaries are contained in F. S. Regs., Part II. and the Staff Manual respectively. Title Pages will be prepared in manuscript.

Place: 105 Hadow

Date	Hour	Summary of Events and Information	Remarks and references to Appendices
		No move. Nothing to Company required. To Fort de TAILLE & return trip to the range.	
		The Company marched to DROUÉ & bivouaced for the night. Preceeding at 5:10 am. with 4 o/c'y. Marched heavily very hot. a great deal of dust.	
		No more used. Cycle advance of the 3rd C.F. MITRAILLEUSES 23e Bataillon	
		1st CHASSEURS ALPIN	
		The MITRAILLEUSE Coys. visited our company. Gen'l behaviour than 1 am & gave a display of drill etc. New shields were cont'd and by us.	
		Transport moved off by road to the CITADEL via DROUÉ	
		The Company marched to HARCOURT, entrained to HERBOIS & marched from there to the CITADEL.	
		The Officers reconnoitred the line from WATERLOT FARM to ARROW HEAD up to Pinn's Farm & Dancing Gun & Wytschaete Corp.	
		Company in reserve.	

WAR DIARY
or
INTELLIGENCE SUMMARY

Army Form C. 2118.

Place	Date	Hour	Summary of Events and Information	Remarks and references to Appendices
	17.9.16		He to be prepared to take part in 1.30pm. (raiding over the long spur from Roclincourt to GUILLEMONT to GUILLEMONT - HARDECOURT road.	
	20.9.16		Hqrs & Bn stragglers remained at the CITADEL. At 1.30pm the 2 Bn was ordered to move up to LANCASTER TRENCH & relieve 11 CHESHIRE Rgt in an attack made starting from the GUILLEMONT-HARDECOURT road & to gain & cover advance from each flank, afterwards to move up to consolidate. Our heavy artillery bombardment from 12 noon to 7 pm its JOURNALS was to open from 7 — 9 pm. Unfortunately the bombardment of the attack. Cheshire's had hardly the men to carry out the attack. The 2 Bn relieved the 11 — 5th Coy complete at 2.30am. Remaining 2 Secs + H.Q. etc moved up to the line.	
	21.9.16		Dispositions — No 2 Sec in line No. 3 in LANCASTER TRENCH No 1 & 4 in supports 150x South of BRIQUETERIE on the BRIQUETERIE - HARDECOURT RA. (4.9pm No 5 & 4 & 1 Sec & Bn H.Q. moved to take up a position in the line from the GUILLEMONT - HARDECOURT road No 2 Sec (LONELY TRENCH). Sunday 15 was + 2 o/r. B Company has relieved. Heavy shelling Shrapnel from enemy MGs. Our own guns shooting short, into a Coy causing the death to infantry.	

Army Form C. 2118.

WAR DIARY
or
INTELLIGENCE SUMMARY

(Erase heading not required.)

Instructions regarding War Diaries and Intelligence Summaries are contained in F. S. Regs., Part II. and the Staff Manual respectively. Title Pages will be prepared in manuscript.

Place	Date	Hour	Summary of Events and Information	Remarks and references to Appendices
			Company marched from dump to SANDPIT VALLEY	
			Company marched to REGINA TRENCH	
			The transport stayed at 11 am in attempts to reach REGINA COURT, spending the night at COURCY	
			On receiving its commander, the company marched to GUEUDECOURT and on to CANADAS ending up in front of a trench running to REGINA COURT.	
			Company marched off on guns and to LUCKNOW ending at 6.30 pm	

105th Machine Gun Coy.

WAR DIARY
or
INTELLIGENCE SUMMARY

Army Form C. 2118.

Place	Date	Hour	Summary of Events and Information	Remarks and references to Appendices
	1-9-16		The Company marched off at 5-15 a.m. to WANQUETIN, arriving at 3 p.m. The O.C. & section officers proceeded at once to ARRAS to reconnoitre the line.	
	2-9-16		The Company proceeded to ARRAS after dark, & arrived at midnight, & billeted for the night.	
	3-9-16		Sections No. 1, 3 & 4 moved up into the line & took over from the 110th M.G. Coy. No. 2 Sec. remained in ARRAS.	12 guns in the line & 4 in reserve.
	4-9-16		The Transport moved from WANQUETIN to DUISANS & took over the lines vacated by the 110th Coy.	
	5-9-16		We were notified that L/Sgt. WILLIAMS had been awarded the Military medal.	
	7-9-16		No. 2 Section relieved No. 4 who came back to ARRAS. One gun used indirect fire during the night.	
	8-9-16		Two guns fired indirect during the night. Target, Nr ST LAURENT-BLANG, the enemy front line. 1500 rounds	
	9-9-16		Indirect fire at night as usual. 1250 "	
	10-9-16		" " " " " "	

Army Form C. 2118.

1/ 105 Machine Gun Coy.

WAR DIARY
or
INTELLIGENCE SUMMARY
(Erase heading not required.)

Instructions regarding War Diaries and Intelligence Summaries are contained in F. S. Regs, Part II. and the Staff Manual respectively. Title Pages will be prepared in manuscript.

Place	Date	Hour	Summary of Events and Information	Remarks and references to Appendices
	11-9-16		No. 4 Section relieved No.1 in the left sector. Indirect fire at night 2500 1250 rounds	
	12-9-16		Usual indirect fire used at night. 1250 rounds	
	13-9-16		2/Lt. J A FRASER appears in orders as having been awarded the military cross. Indirect fire 1500 rounds	
	14-9-16		A raid was carried out by the 15th CHESHIRE regt. On our right. 2/Lt. fm. guns assisted with indirect fire & 1 min guns continued to fire during the night. One gun (704) M.G. Coy, which is in our right, cooperated with us 8700 rounds.	
	15-9-16		No.1 section relieved No.3 in the left sector. Indirect fire 4,450. On the night of 15/16 our Artillery bombarded the enemy as a diversion while the 104 Brigade made a raid. Our guns cooperated with in direct fire.	
	16-9-16			
	17-9-16		Indirect fire at night. 1000 rounds	
	19-9-16		No. 3 sec. relieved No.2 in the right sector. Indirect fire - 1250 rounds.	
	20-9-16		Indirect fire - 750 rounds.	
	21-9-16		" " 2600 "	

3/ 105 Machine Gun Company -

Army Form C. 2118.

WAR DIARY
or
INTELLIGENCE SUMMARY
(Erase heading not required.)

Place	Date	Hour	Summary of Events and Information	Remarks and references to Appendices
	22-9-16		Indirect fire 4500 rounds	
	23-9-16		" " 1000 "	
	24-9-16		" " 1000 "	
	25-9-16		" " 2000 "	
	26-9-16		" " 1000 "	
	27-9-16		No 4 section relieved No 1 Indirect fire 1000	
	28-9-16		Indirect fire 500	
	29-9-16		" " 1750	
	30-9-16		" " 2000	

Instructions regarding War Diaries and Intelligence Summaries are contained in F. S. Regs., Part II. and the Staff Manual respectively. Title Pages will be prepared in manuscript.

Army Form C. 2118.

WAR DIARY
or
INTELLIGENCE SUMMARY
(Erase heading not required.)

Instructions regarding War Diaries and Intelligence Summaries are contained in F. S. Regs, Part II. and the Staff Manual respectively. Title Pages will be prepared in manuscript.

Place	Date	Hour	Summary of Events and Information	Remarks and references to Appendices
In the Field	Sept 1st		Coy marched from LUCHEUX to WANQUETIN arriving 3 pm.	
	2nd		Coy marched to ARRAS, arrived 12 noon 2/3rd Sept, & relieved Relieving 110 M. Gun Coy in the line. 1, 3 & 4 Sections in the line.	
	3rd		Not in Reserve. Ordinary Trench warfare.	
	4th		Transport moved from WANQUETIN to DUISANS.	
	5th			
	6th to 13th		Ordinary trench warfare. Enemy mortared his own trenches. Raided by 15th Cheshires, partially successful, secured 4 prisoners.	
	14th			
	15th to 30th		Ordinary trench warfare. Section doing 12 days in the line & 4 out. Indirect fire nearly every night about 3,900 rounds fired during the month. A lot of work done improving dug-outs & emplacements.	

A J Nelson Major
O.C. 105 M. Gun Coy

2449 Wt. W14957/M90 750,000 1/16 J.B.C. & A. Forms/C.2118/12.

Army Form C. 2118.

V o2 6

105 Machine Gun Coy.

WAR DIARY
or
INTELLIGENCE SUMMARY
(Erase heading not required.)

Instructions regarding War Diaries and Intelligence Summaries are contained in F. S. Regs., Part II. and the Staff Manual respectively. Title Pages will be prepared in manuscript.

Place	Date	Hour	Summary of Events and Information	Remarks and references to Appendices
ARRAS	Oct 1/18	1	No. 3 section was relieved by No. 1. Indirect fire 2000	
		2	Ordinary trench work. Indirect fire 7000 rounds.	
		3		
		4		
		5	No. 3 section relieved No. 2	
		6	Indirect fire 7750 rounds	
		7		
		8	106? Bde. on left & 104? on right discharged gas at 8-45 pm. and we cooperated with Indirect fire - 5500 rounds.	
		9	No. 2 Sect. relieved No. 4. Indirect fire 1250 rounds.	
		10	Indirect fire 8500 rounds	
		11		
		12		
		13	No. 4 sect. relieved No. 1. Indirect fire 3500 rounds	
		14	Indirect fire 4750 rounds.	
		15		
		16		

Army Form C. 2118.

WAR DIARY
or
INTELLIGENCE SUMMARY
(Erase heading not required.)

2 / 105 Machine Gun Coy.

Instructions regarding War Diaries and Intelligence Summaries are contained in F. S. Regs., Part II and the Staff Manual respectively. Title Pages will be prepared in manuscript.

Place	Date	Hour	Summary of Events and Information	Remarks and references to Appendices
ARRAS	Oct. 1916	17	No. 1 section relieved No. 3. No indirect fire.	
		18	} Indirect fire 1000 rounds.	
		19		
		20		
		21	No. 3 sect. relieved No. 2. — At night of 21/22 15/16 CHESHIRES raided the co-operated with in direct fire — 8625 rounds.	
		22	} Indirect fire 4000 rounds.	
		23		
		24		
		25	No. 2 section relieved No. 4 in 16 right section. At 8 pm 16 15th SHERWOODS raided the enemy trenches. Our prisoners was brought back. We co-operated with indirect fire on usual targets, especially BLANGY villages & trenches in rear of raided area — 12,000 rounds. The prisoner reports that our indirect fire has caused great inconvenience to the enemy. We have caused many casualties on the BLANGY road & rendered communication trench unfit for traffic.	

2449 Wt. W14957/M90 750,000 1/16 J.B.C. & A. Forms/C.2118/12.

3/ 105th Machine Gun Coy.

Army Form C. 2118.

WAR DIARY
or
INTELLIGENCE SUMMARY
(Erase heading not required.)

Instructions regarding War Diaries and Intelligence Summaries are contained in F. S. Regs., Part II. and the Staff Manual respectively. Title Pages will be prepared in manuscript.

Place	Date	Hour	Summary of Events and Information	Remarks and references to Appendices
ARRAS	Oct 1916	26 27	Indirect fire 1700 rounds.	
		28	From examination of a German prisoner we learned that the enemy were relieving in the evening. Indirect fire was used in communication trenches & approaches generally. 23,250 rounds were expended.	
		29	No. 4 Section relieved No. 1. No indirect fire.	
		30 31	No Indirect fire. A great deal of work has been done by the Coy. on new emplacements & dugouts during the month.	

Original

WAR DIARY or INTELLIGENCE SUMMARY

105 Machine Gun Company Army Form C. 2118.

Place	Date	Hour	Summary of Events and Information	Remarks and references to Appendices
In the Field	1916 Nov 1		Trench warfare. Indirect fire 9,000 rounds	
	2		Enemy bombarded front line. Retaliation with T.M's. etc. One gun co-operated at 4 P.M. Indirect fire 5,250 rounds	
	3		Establishment of M.G. Coys having been increased 33 men per Infantry Battalion in Bde. transferred to this company	
			Enemy relief suspected, indirect fire was used on his trenches/communication during its height. Total rounds fired 114,000	
	4		Indirect fire 2000 rounds	
	5		Indirect fire 1000 "	
	6		No 2 Section relieved No 2 Section. Indirect fire 2,500 rounds	
	7		Indirect fire 1,500 rounds	
	8		Indirect fire 2,750 rounds	
	9		Indirect fire 1,500 rounds	
	10		No 3 Section relieved No 4 in left sector. Indirect fire 3000 rounds	
	11		Indirect fire 3000 rounds	
	12		" " 7,000 "	
	13		" " 6,750 "	
	14		" " 2,500 " No 4 Section relieved No 1. During ablutions + 4 T.M. shafts guns fired on BLANGY VILLAGE	
	15		" " 5,500 "	
	16		" " 4,000 "	
	17		" " 2,500 "	
	18		" " 2,000 " No 1 Section relieved No 3	
	19		" " 5,500 "	
	20		" " 3,250 "	
	21		" " 4,750 "	
	22		" " 1,000 " No 3 Section relieved No 2	
	23		" " 4,250 " Targets ALT2, TRAUM + SALZACH TRENCHES	
	24		" " 10,000 "	
	25		" " 3,050 " Target BLANGY VILLAGE and communication trenches	

WAR DIARY
or
INTELLIGENCE SUMMARY

(Erase heading not required.)

105 Machine Gun Company, Army Form C. 2118.

Place	Date	Hour	Summary of Events and Information	Remarks and references to Appendices
In the Field	1916 Nov 26		Enemy attempted to rush our trenches, indirect fire from 3-30 A.M. until daylight 7000 rounds	
	27		Indirect fire 5,500 rounds. No 2 Section relieved No 4 in Centre Sector	
	28		" " 2,000 "	
	29		" " 4,000 "	
	30		" " 3,500 "	

A.J. Foden Major
OC 105 M.G. Coy

105 Machine Gun Company

WAR DIARY
or
INTELLIGENCE SUMMARY
(Erase heading not required.)

Army Form C. 2118.

105 M G Coy

Vol 4

Place	Date	Hour	Summary of Events and Information	Remarks and references to Appendices
	Dec. 1 1916		Trench strafes. Indirect fire 6000 rounds.	
	2		"	
	3		Company relieved by 26 Machine Gun Company & marched to AGNEZ.	
	4		Company moved to new billets at IZEL les HAMEAU.	
	5		Billets inspected by G.O.C. 105 Inf. Bde.	
	6		Company training	
	7		Billets inspected by G.O.C. 35th Division	
	8		Company training	
	9		"	
	10		Brigade church parade at MANIN.	
	11		Company training	
	12		No 2 Section relieved 111 Company at Anti-aircraft posts AVESNES le COMPTE	
	13		Lecture by 35th Div. Gas Expert	
	14		Company training	
	15		Rifle & revolver shooting	
	16		Brigade church parade at MANIN.	
	17		Company training	
	18		"	
	19			
	20			
	21			
	22		Inspection by G.O.C. 35th Div.	
	23		Company training	
	24		Bde. football competition	
	25		Xmas day.	
	26		Bde. shooting competition at AMBRIVES.	
	27		Company moved to LATTRE St QUENTIN	
	28		Company training	
	29		"	
	30			
	31			

A J Miller Maj
O C 105 M G Coy.

Army Form C. 2118.

105 Machine Gun Company

105 M G Coy

Vol 9

WAR DIARY
or
INTELLIGENCE SUMMARY

(Erase heading not required.)

Instructions regarding War Diaries and Intelligence Summaries are contained in F. S. Regs., Part II. and the Staff Manual respectively. Title Pages will be prepared in manuscript.

Place	Date	Hour	Summary of Events and Information	Remarks and references to Appendices
In the Field	1917 Jan 1		Inspection by G.O.C. 105 Inf. Bde.	
	2		Company training	
	3			
	4			
	5		Transport inspection by 105 Inf Bde. Commander.	
	6		Company training	
	7			
	8			
	9			
	10		Company training. D Coy M G O inspected Company	
	11			
	12		Company training	
	13			
	14			
	15			
	16		Company training. Inspection by M.O. for scabies	
	17		Company training	
	18		Company moved by road to MONTS en TERNOIS	
	19			
	20			
	21			
	22		Company training	
	23			
	24			
	25			
	26		Company training. 25 men working under R.E. officer in MONTS en TERNOIS & BUNEVILLE.	
	27			
	28			
	29			
	30			
	31		Company moved by road to HOUVIN HOUVIGNEUL.	

J. S. Lang Lt /a
O.C. 105 Machine Gun Coy.

Army Form C. 2118.

105 M G Coy

Vol 10

WAR DIARY
~~INTELLIGENCE SUMMARY.~~
(Erase heading not required.)

Instructions regarding War Diaries and Intelligence Summaries are contained in F.S. Regs., Part II. and the Staff Manual respectively. Title pages will be prepared in manuscript.

Place	Date	Hour	Summary of Events and Information	Remarks and references to Appendices
HOUVIN-MOUVIGNEUL	1/2/17 – 5/2/17		Coy Training	
	6/2/17		Coy moved by road to BONNIERS.	
	7/2/17		" " " " LONGUEVILLETTE.	
	8/2/17		" " " " FRÉMONT.	
FRÉMONT	9–17/2/17		Coy Training	
	18/2/17		Coy Trained to DEMUIN.	
DEMUIN	19/2/17		Coy Training	
	20/2/17		Coy relieved M.G. Coys of the 1st & 3rd Batts & 16th Regt. + a Coy of the 15th Bn of the 413th Regt. of the 154th French Division.	
	21/2/17		Trench Warfare. Boche discharged gas on the left. Three of our guns opened fire.	
	22/2/17		Trench Warfare	
	23–26/2/17		Trench Warfare	
	27/2/17		Trench Warfare	
	28/2/17		Trench Warfare	

JBSholden Lieut for Major
Commanding 105 MG Company.

WAR DIARY or INTELLIGENCE SUMMARY

Army Form C. 2118.

105 Machine Gun Coy.   105 M.G. Coy.

Instructions regarding War Diaries and Intelligence Summaries are contained in F.S. Regs., Part II. and the Staff Manual respectively. Title Pages will be prepared in manuscript.

(Erase heading not required.)

Place	Date	Hour	Summary of Events and Information	Remarks and references to Appendices
CHILLY SECTOR	March 1	1	Trench warfare.	
		2	Enemy raided. 2nd gun opened fire.	
		3	Enemy raided. Guns in front & second line opened fire. One gun hit by shell fire & damaged.	
		4	Trench warfare.	
		5	"	
		6	"	
		7	Company relieved by 104 M.G. Coy. Company moved to billets in ROSIERES.	
		8	Company moved to new billets CAIX.	
		9	Company training.	
		10	" Guns mounted for against aircraft attack.	
		11	Company training	
		12	" No 3 section attacked to R.n. Cheshire Regt. for practice attack.	
		13	"	
		14	" Section officers reconnoitred LIHONS Sector. No 4 section att. to M Glos Regt for practice attack	
		15	Company marched to ROSIERS & relieved 116 M.G. Coy in LIHONS sector.	
		16	Ordinary Trench warfare.	
		17	Indirect fire by 8 guns on selected trench spots in approximation artillery from 7am to 7.45am. at 7pm. 8 guns moved forward to German front line which had been evacuated that afternoon. Against sections moved from ROSIERS to positions	
			in LUNETTE II.	
		18	Four guns moved forward to position in new front line in German second system of trenches. Remaining twelve guns? concentrated with battalion in support.	
		19	16 guns concentrated at HYENCOURT le PETIT.	
		20	Transport moved to HYENCOURT le PETIT. Transport moved from CAIX to ROSIERS.	
		21	One section detached to 4th section. On line as permanent working party. Remainder of Company training.	
		22	Three sections working at CURCHY.	
		23	Four officers & 60 men working under R.E. officer on railway construction. CHAULNES – NESTLE line.	

Army Form C. 2118.

105 Machine Gun Coy.

WAR DIARY
or
INTELLIGENCE SUMMARY

(Erase heading not required.)

Instructions regarding War Diaries and Intelligence Summaries are contained in F. S. Regs., Part II. and the Staff Manual respectively. Title Pages will be prepared in manuscript.

Place	Date	Hour	Summary of Events and Information	Remarks and references to Appendices
HYENCOURT LE PETIT	April 24		One section detachment working with one line between remainder of Company of railway construction work	
	25		" " "	
	26		" " "	
	27		" " "	
	28		" " "	
	29			
	30			
	31			

J. E. Lang Lt. I/c
O.C. 105 Machine Gun Coy.

105 Machine Gun Company. **WAR DIARY** *or* **INTELLIGENCE SUMMARY**

Army Form C. 2118.

105 M.G. Coy
Vol 12

Place	Date	Hour	Summary of Events and Information	Remarks and references to Appendices
1917				
HYENCOURT le PETIT	April 1		Company moved to MESNIL le PETIT. Orders received that Company was to be prepared to move at four hours notice.	
MESNIL le PETIT	2		Company less one section attached to 4th An Line Section working on CHAULNES – NESTLE railway.	
"	3		Company less one section moved to billets in HOMBLEUX.	
HOMBLEUX	4		Three sections provided day and night working party for 24 hours on tunnel under CHAULNES-NESTLE railway embankment.	
"	5		Company training.	
"	6		Open warfare attack practice with 15th Cheshire Regt	
"	7		Open warfare attack practice with 16th Cheshire Regt	
"	8		Co-operated with 15th Sherwoods, attack practice on village of CANIZY.	
"	9		Practice barrage on village of YOYENNES.	
"	10		Open warfare attack practice with 4th Gloucester Regt	
"	11		Company training. Section attached to 4th Ain Line section returned to Head Quarters.	
"	12		Company moved to MERANCOURT.	
MERANCOURT	13		Company moved to VILLEVEQUE and was attached to 104 Inf Bde.	
VILLEVEQUE.	14		Cleaning belts etc.	
	15		Company moved to VILLECHOLLES. The village of PONTRUET was to be raided on morning of April 16, and orders were received that the Lewis guns of the Company were to fire on the village and put a barrage on roads in the hearing. The Company moved to positions by attached sketches pushing on shell no. positions shown on attached map.	
	16		Zero being fixed for 3am at that hour the Lewis guns of the Company opened fire and formed a barrage on road marked I on attached map. At 0.45 minutes gun of Nos. 1, 2 & 3 sections lifted to road marked II and from Nº 4 Section one chief track marked III. At 0.20 all guns ceased fire and the Company returned to billets at VILLECHOLLES. The raiding party went night through the village and captured no persons. In the evening the Company moved to H.Q. hut and attached 104 Machine Gun Company.	
	17		Semi-Open Warfare	
	18		"	
	19		"	
	20		"	
	21		"	
	22		It having been discovered that the triangle of roads east side of PONTRUET was being occupied and used as a strong point by the enemy, bursts of artillery fire were brought to bear on it at the following hours. 9.15 pm 9.45 pm 10.20 pm 11.15 pm 2 & 5 am and 5.10 am	

Army Form C. 2118.

105 Machine Gun Coy.

WAR DIARY
INTELLIGENCE SUMMARY
(Erase heading not required.)

Instructions regarding War Diaries and Intelligence Summaries are contained in F. S. Regs., Part II. and the Staff Manual respectively. Title Pages will be prepared in manuscript.

Place	Date 1917	Hour	Summary of Events and Information	Remarks and references to Appendices
	April 22		All these hours indirect fire was brought to bear on the same target from positions M.26.6.9.0 and M.26.6.S.2. Positions as shown on attached map. In defence of sectors were selected, work on emplacements at these positions continued. Semi-open warfare.	
	23		"	
	24		"	
	25		"	
	26		"	
	27		The 59th Division attacked a line of trenches in their sector. The 36th Div. co-operated with artillery and machine gun barrage demonstration. Four guns (No II Section) fired from a point M.15.d.1.2. in front of their trenches near ST HELENE and on the road from ST HELENE to PORTRUET. Zero was fixed for 3.53 A.M. and firing was continued until 0+15 minutes. Semi Open warfare.	
	28		Company relieved by 106 M.G. Coy - on completion of relief Coy moved to VILLEVEQUE.	
	29			
VILLEVEQUE	30		Company cleaning + overhauling all guns belts + equipment.	

A Parker
O.C 105 M.G.Coy

1/5/17

Army Form C. 2118.

WAR DIARY
or
INTELLIGENCE SUMMARY

105th Machine Gun Company

Vol 13

Place	Date 1917	Hour	Summary of Events and Information	Remarks and references to Appendices
VILLEVEQUE	May 1		Reference Maps 62 B. S.W. 1/20,000 Company training	
	2		"	
	3		"	
	4		Anti-aircraft gun mounted at W.9.t.o.9	
	5		76 men working on trails in Q.29 on POEUILLY-VERMAND Rd. VILLECHOLLES Rd. Company bathed. On evening two sections moved to the R to remount the attack. No 1 Section traversed ground ahead the guns g 106 M G bn to the (near line during the attack) two guns in conjunction in barrage placed from M.2.a. & M.7d.23 (forward edge of copse) all guns withdrawn from the line at 3 A.M.	
	6		No 3 Section ten men on a.a. duty. Supporting in attack practice with 15th Cheshires. No. 4 Section in parallels in attack practice with 15th Cheshires Regt.	
	7		Ten men filling in trails in Q.29 on POEUILLY-VERMAND Rd.	
	8		Preparing for line.	
	9		Company relieved 106 M.G. Coy in line. Company headquarters moved to VILLECHOLLES R.33.a.1.9.	
	10		Trenchart Company Headquarters shelled out of VILLECHOLLES, moved to R.33.a.1.9. Indirect fire by No guns by No 1 Section + 2 guns by No 2 section on MONIDEE during the night.	
MARTEVILLE	11		Coy Head Quarters + transport moved to R.32.d.6.7 (near MARTEVILLE).	
	12		Small Open warfare	
	13		15 stragglers attempted to raid LES TROIS SAUVAGES. Zero hour was fixed in barrage at 10 guns 1) 105 MG Coy fired at pinning target No. 2 section +guns on S.9 FRESNOY target hands from M.24 c.S.6 & M.24.a.m.7 No 1 section targets 2 guns on C.T from M.26.c.S.6 & M.24.d.2.6 2guns on trenches M.24 a.m. 7 to M.24.a.6.0 No 3 Section targets, 2 guns on road from M.24.a.7.0 to M.14 a.c.2. Rate of fire 0 to c+30 1 belt per gun per minute. 0+30 to 0+60 1 half per gun per 6 minute. The road was not successful. 3 guns g 106 M.G. Gy under K. FISHER attached to this unit (the remainder of the Company having been relieved by 5th Company) Division (Canadian Divn).	

2449 Wt. W14957/M90 750,000 1/16 J.B.C. & A. Forms/C.2118/12.

Army Form C. 2118.

"105" Machine Gun Cy

WAR DIARY
or
INTELLIGENCE SUMMARY
(Erase heading not required.)

Instructions regarding War Diaries and Intelligence Summaries are contained in F. S. Regs., Part II. and the Staff Manual respectively. Title Pages will be prepared in manuscript.

Place	Date 1917	Hour	Summary of Events and Information	Remarks and references to Appendices
	May 16		Some gun practice	
	17		Artillery shelled LES TROIS SAUVAGES from 2.45 am to 3.30 am 10 guns of this company fired on enemy line road & 15 shrapnels on night of 15-16 May.	
	18		Officers of 87th French division reconnoitred the line	
	19		Company relieved by 87th French division. 1 N.C.O & section was left in H.Q. line until relieving M.G. Coy. The Company moved to TREFCON	
TREFCON	20		Cleaning guns, ammunition etc	
	21		Company training	
	22		Company training in morning, sports in afternoon against 15th Cheshire Regt afternoon N.C.O, WI & NR French attend K Coy	
	23		Company moved by road to PERONNE.	
PERONNE	24		Cleaning guns equipment etc.	
	25		Company moved to Camp East of SOREL le GRAND	
SOREL le GRAND	26		Company moved to AIZECOURT le BAS	
AIZECOURT le BAS	27		Company training	
	28		" " 2 anti-aircraft guns mounted. N°1 section & portion of transport inoculated	
	29		organised parties	
	30		Company training N°2 section mounted.	
	31		N°3 section inoculated. Company training. N°1 section acting as enemy to specified anti battalion in attack practice, left A & B section second edrs E moved to Gouillecourt	

J. S. Lang Lt /n
O.C. 105 Machine Gun Coy

Army Form C. 2118.

WAR DIARY
or
INTELLIGENCE SUMMARY

105 M G Coy

Vol 14

(Erase heading not required.)

Instructions regarding War Diaries and Intelligence Summaries are contained in F. S. Regs., Part II. and the Staff Manual respectively. Title Pages will be prepared in manuscript.

Place	Date 1917	Hour	Summary of Events and Information	Remarks and references to Appendices
AIZECOURT LE BAS.	June 1		Coll. P.R. Waite P. & 6/ KNVR. took over command of the Coy. Company relieved 106 M.G. Coy	
VILLERS GUISLAIN.	2-7		in the VILLERS-GUISLAIN sector of the Divisional front. Trench warfare.	
	8		Trench Warfare. Transport inspected by G.O.C. 36th Division	
	9-14		Trench warfare.	
	15		Trench warfare. Quartette transport materiel.	
	16		Trench warfare.	
	17		Relieved by 104 M.G. Coy. Coy moved to billets in AZIECOURT LE BAS.	
AZIECOURT LE BAS	18		Rest.	
	19-21		Training	
	22		Drawing 29 men from No1 section + 5 from No 2 sect. proceeded to Bussu for Haymaking.	
	23-24		Drawing.	
GAUCHE WOOD	25		Coy relieved 106 M.G. Coy in GAUCHE WOOD section of Divisional front.	
	26-30		Trench warfare.	

JR Shute Lt. [?]
105 Machine Gun Company

105 M.G. Coy
Vol 15

WAR DIARY
INTELLIGENCE SUMMARY
(Erase heading not required.)

Army Form C. 2118.

Place	Date	Hour	Summary of Events and Information	Remarks and references to Appendices
DRIECHE WOOD	July 1		Company relieved by 121 Company - 6 guns only taken over	
VILLERS FAUCON	2		Cleaning up + training	
"	3,4,5		Training	
"	6		On the night of the 6-7th the Coy relieved the M. Guns of the 3rd Cavalry Squadron in D sector of the Divisional front.	
EPHEY	7 to 12		Trench warfare.	
"	13		3h Cavalry Squadron attached on return to BIRDCAGE - shown in various M.G. positions, to the overall barrage lines of our guns.	
ALBECOURT & BAS	14		Coy relieved by 184 Coy & moved to ALBECOURT & BAS.	
"	15		Clean guns etc.	
"	16		Training	
"	17		Travelling workshops by G.O.C. 35th Div - Result satisfactory - Training	
"	18-19		Training	
"	20		Section Officers reconnoitred new line - Training	
"	21		Training	
"	22		Relieved 106 Coy in GUILLEMONT FARM Sector of Div Front.	
ST EMILIE	23-29		Trench warfare.	
"	30		"	
"	31		Divided fire theough line taken.	

Godshall Lt
105 Machine Gun Coy.

Army Form C. 2118.

August 1917

105 M.G. Coy

Vol 16

WAR DIARY
INTELLIGENCE SUMMARY
(Erase heading not required.)

Instructions regarding War Diaries and Intelligence Summaries are contained in F. S. Regs., Part II. and the Staff Manual respectively. Title Pages will be prepared in manuscript.

Place	Date	Hour	Summary of Events and Information	Remarks and references to Appendices
ST. EMILIE	1-9-17		Trench Warfare	
	2-9-17		Coy relieved by 106th M.G. Coy	
HIZECOURT-LE-BAS	3-9-17 – 9-9-17		Company training.	
	10-9-17		No 1 Section relieved 2 guns of 106th M.G. Coy	
	11-9-17		12 New Nos 2,3rd Sections digging barrage emplacements	
	12-9-17		Brigade practice attack	
	13-9-17		Relief of men at work on barrage emplacements	
	14-9-17		Company training & preparation of barrage emplacements	
	15-9-17		Brigade practice attack.	
	16-9-17		Coy training & preparing to go into the line	
	17-9-17		Coy moved to Barrage Positions	
	18-9-17		Preparation for attack	
	19-9-17		Attack on KNOLL 4.0 AM successful. C.P. guns 9.40 + 11 AM guns fired on S.O.S. line	
	20-9-17		C.P. 9AM & 2.45 PM gun fired on S.O.S line	
	21-9-17		Unsuccessful Counter attack by "Boche" at 3.57AM from 4 points	
	22-9-17 – 24-9-17		Trench Warfare	
	25-9-17		"Boche" Counter attack on GUILLEMONT FARM opened fire on S.O.S. line	
	26-9-17		Trench Warfare	
	27-9-17		Brigade relieved by 106th Inf Bde, with the exception of M.G. Coy.	
	28-9-17 – 29-9-17		Trench Warfare	
EPÉHY	30-9-17		"Boche" Counter attack on KNOLL guns opened fire on S.O.S. line.	
	31-9-17		Trench Warfare	

John G Fraser Lt for O.C.
105 Ch. M.G. Coy.

No. 105 M.G. COY.
Date 8.9.17

Army Form C. 2118.

WAR DIARY
or
INTELLIGENCE SUMMARY
(Erase heading not required.)

105 M.G. Archive Gun Company

Vol 17

No. 105 M.G. Coy.
Date 3.10.17

Place	Date Sept	Hour	Summary of Events and Information	Remarks and references to Appendices
LEMPIRE ROAD	1		Trench Warfare. No 4 Section relieved by Section of 241st M.G Coy. 106 M.G Bde returned to 105 M.G Coy	
	2	12.10 AM	S.O.S. Cologne Farm and Gillemont Farm	
	3-4-5		Trench Warfare	
	6		Boche "Strafed" by M.G's.	
	7		Trench Warfare	
	8		Boche Strafed for 20 mins by F.A. & M.G's. no retaliation	
	9		Boche Counter attacked. Dis. a. mgt (Sur.Boy) Coy H.P. move to ST EMILIE	
ST EMILIE	10		Trench Warfare. half minute "Strafe" in conjunction with artillery	
	11		Trench Warfare	
	12-13		Coy relieved by two section 104 Bde M.G. Coy & two sections of 241 ST M.G Coy. & proceeded to AIZECOURT-LE-BAS after having held the line for 25 days.	
AIZECOURT-LE-BAS	13		Coy Training - cleaning up. Transport moved in to M.G. Coy took over stores	
	14-15		Training	
	16		Annual Parade	
	17-		Training	
	18		Distribution of awards by Corps Commander. Coy congratulated for its good work in recent operations	
PARAS BANK NURLU	19-20		Coy relieved 106 Bde M.G. Coy in "D" Sector Div front.	
			Trench Warfare.	
	20-21		" " in section of N.G.S. & T.M.S. Lt. WHEELER attached E.O of 245 Bn. A. Cy.	
	22		" " continued short of N.G.S & T.M.S attached E.O. of 245 Bn.A.Cy.	
	23		" " in conjunction with raid in KNOLL by 105th Bde on an mgt.	
	24		" " by 4'ys placed in conjunction with a T.M's firing incendiary bombs, 18 Rhos & Heavy	
	25		" " held in HONN ECOURT WOOD in conjunction with 7 x & M/Pde No 6 Bn. and L.Y.	
	26-28		Artillery also fired on a dummy in front of GONNELIEU by 7 x & M/Pde No 6 Bn. and L.Y.	
	29		Trench Warfare.	
	27-30		Trench Warfare. C.O. & 2 Officers of 166 Bde M.G Coy (55 Div) reconnoitred the line preliminary to taking over	
	30		No 4 Section relieved by section of 166 M.G Coy	
	30 Sept - 1 Oct		Trench Warfare. Remainder of Coy relieved by 166 Bde M.G. Coy. A quick + good relief. On relief company proceeded
			To AIZECOURT-LE-BAS	

John O. Fraser & Lt for Capt. A.
Comdg. 105 M.G Coy

Vol 18

War Diary
of
No. 105 M.G. Coy.
for
October, 1917.

Army Form C. 2118.

WAR DIARY
or
INTELLIGENCE SUMMARY

(Erase heading not required.)

Instructions regarding War Diaries and Intelligence Summaries are contained in F. S. Regs., Part II. and the Staff Manual respectively. Title Pages will be prepared in manuscript.

Place	Date	Hour	Summary of Events and Information	Remarks and references to Appendices
PERONNE.	Oct. 1.		Company proceeded to PERONNE.	
	2.		Billets at PERONNE.	
	3.		Transport marched to BAPAUME.	
	4.		Company proceeded by rail to ARRAS, and marched to DAINVILLE. Transport arrived later.	
DAINVILLE.	5.		Interior Training	
	6.		ditto	
	7.		ditto	
	8.		ditto	
	9.		ditto	
	10.		ditto	
	11.		ditto	
ARRAS.	12.		Company entrained at ARRAS for CASSEL (O.O. attached)	
LEDRINGHEM	13.		marched to billets in LEDRINGHEM, near ARNEKE.	
			10 O.R. attached to the company from 14 th Bn. GLOUCESTER Regt. 11 from 13 th Bn. CHESHIRE Regt. and 11 from 16 th CHESHIRE Regt. as carriers. Guns tested.	
	14.		Company moved by rail, transport by road from ARNEKE to PROVEN, billeted in PEQUELLcamp.	
PROVEN.	15.		Company moved as before (O.O. attached) from PROVEN to EMILE farm, near ELVERDINGHE.	
ELVERDINGHE	16.		Company in support to 104 th (Inf) Bde. at WOOD 15. Returned at daylight.	
	17.		Resting	
	18.		Reconnaissance preparatory to going in line.	
	19.		Company takes over line from 106 th M.G. Coy. One section in front, one in barrage position, attached to	
	20.		241 st (Divisional) Coy. one in reserve. One section prepared to consolidate ground taken by infantry in attack next morning. 2/Lt JONES wounded during relief. 2 3 O.R. casualties.	
	21.		2/Lt FURMSTON wounded	
	22.		Supporting section successfully consolidated ground won during operations on Spds of HOUTHULST FOREST. Three guns in front line and two in forward position of Right.	

2449 Wt. W14957/M90 750,000 1/16 J.B.C. & A. Forms/C.2118/12.

Army Form C. 2118.

WAR DIARY
or
INTELLIGENCE SUMMARY

(Erase heading not required.)

Instructions regarding War Diaries and Intelligence Summaries are contained in F. S. Regs., Part II. and the Staff Manual respectively. Title Pages will be prepared in manuscript.

Place	Date	Hour	Summary of Events and Information	Remarks and references to Appendices
BOSINGHE	23.		Uneventful: Front line sections relieved by a section of 241st M.G. Coy. Section on relief proceeded to BOSINGHE.	
	24.		Resting. Lt FRASER appointed second in command, vice Lt WHEELER.	
	25.		Company relieved 241st company with one section in the front line. 3 sections marched to BOXCAR.	
	26.		Refitting. Barrage section relieved by 106th M.G. Coy.	
	27.		Refilling ammunition &c.	
	28.		Continue Refitting. Draft of 41 men from base.	
	29.		Inspection by Major General Commanding 3rd Division. 2/Lt STAINTON joined the company.	
	30.		During the operations the company received fifty seven casualties including officers.	
	31.		Company Training. Construction	

Army Form C. 2118.

WAR DIARY
or
INTELLIGENCE SUMMARY / 105th Machine Gun Company.

Vol 19

(Erase heading not required.)

Instructions regarding War Diaries and Intelligence Summaries are contained in F. S. Regs., Part II. and the Staff Manual respectively. Title Pages will be prepared in manuscript.

Place	Date	Hour	Summary of Events and Information	Remarks and references to Appendices
J. CAMP. near WOETEN	Nov 1917 1		Coy Training & Construction of A.A. emplacements.	
	2-4		Coy Training & Construction of Horse Standings	
	5		Coy moved by train to PROVEN area entraining at ORBINK. Firs fort moved mo[u]nted.	
PALISTOWE CAMP Nr. PROVEN	6		Completion of 105th M.G.Coy by Div. Commander.	
	7-14		Coy Training	
	15		Coy moved by train to BROWNE Camp entraining at PROVEN transport moved by road. Relieved 173rd M.G. Coy in Divisional Reserve.	
BROWNE Camp Nr. POPERINGHE	16-22		Coy Training.	
	23		Officers reconnoitred the line.	
	24		Coy marched to KEMPTON PARK & relieved 108th M.G. Coy in the line	
KEMPTON PARK	25-28		Trench Warfare	
	29		Coy relieved by 106th M.G. Coy & proceeded to SIEGE Camp. Relieved ELVIS IN CHIEF, MARM ERTINGHE.	
SIEGE Camp	30		Cleaning guns etc.	

Latham Hutton Capt.
Comdg 105th M.G. Coy

2449 Wt. W14957/M90 750,000 1/16 J.B.C. & A. Forms/C.2118/12.

WAR DIARY or INTELLIGENCE SUMMARY

Army Form C. 2118.

105th MACHINE GUN COMPANY.

1.10.17 to 31.10.17

Volume 2

Place	Date Oct 1917	Hour	Summary of Events and Information	Remarks and references to Appendices
SIEGE CAMP	1-3		Company Training & Reconnoitring the line.	
	4		" "	
	5		8 guns relieved 8 guns of 50th Machine Gun Company on the left of Nieuport front.	
	6		Remaining 8 guns relieved 24155 Machine Gun Company, having 14 guns in front line & 2 in reserve.	
	7		Trench warfare.	
	8		Coy relieved by 214th M.G. Coy in reserve & 215 M.G. Coy in the line.	
LE NOUVEAU MONDE	9		Coy moved by road, transport by road, to NOUVEAU MONDE in the HOUTKERQUE area.	
	10		Coy Training.	
POPERINGHE	11		Coy moved by road to SCHOOLS CAMP near POPERINGHE, Corps Reserve.	
	12		Cleaning Limbers & equipment. 90R. per Battn. attached permanently to this Coy. from 15th & 16th Cheshire and 13th Sherwoods.	
	13/14		Coy Training. New Box Respirators Containers fitted.	
	15		Coy Training. 90R. attached permanently from 14th Gloster.	
	16		Bde. Church Service.	
	17		Coy Training.	
	18		" Bde Sports commence. Coy beat T.M.Bty. at football.	
	19-22		" "	
	23		Church Parade	
	24		Coy Training. No. 4 Section won Bde. revolver (O.R.) competition.	
	25		Xmas festivities. 100 O.R. from Coy. dined in POPERINGHE at "LA POUPÉE" restaurant.	
	26		" " " " "	
	27-31		Coy Training.	

C. Fraser Hunt
Comdg. 105 M.G. Coy.

Army Form C. 2118.

60th MACHINE GUN COMPANY

WAR DIARY
or
INTELLIGENCE SUMMARY

Jan 1st – 31st 1916

Volume II

(Erase heading not required.)

Instructions regarding War Diaries and Intelligence Summaries are contained in F. S. Regs., Part II. and the Staff Manual respectively. Title Pages will be prepared in manuscript.

Place	Date	Hour	Summary of Events and Information	Remarks and references to Appendices
SCHOOL CAMP	1st		Football v 15th Sherwoods.	
	2nd–4th		Coy Training	
	5		Church Parade	
	6		Transport Inspection by Major Gen. G. M. FRANKS, C.B.	
	7		Coy Training	
	8			
	9		March PESO. FERINO CAMP. ENTRAINING & Transport by road march to MOASCAR and Train BELVERDING HSE.
SOLIFERINO CAMP	10/Jan 2		Coy Training	
	3		Church Parade	
	4–11/6		Coy Training	
	12		Coy Parade	
KEMPTON PARK	13		Coy Park order on train from 10th Bde Coy Trains to KEMPTON PARK. Twelve guns on the line. No 4 Section sure	
	14		NH is a post-condition of destroying the journey should it get into their hands if can give terms on reference up roads fortunes 9/8 NO 12, 13, 14 and 15 what a given	
	15			
	16			
	17			
	18		Clean day. Removed watering, watering on PROGRESS STATES	
	19		Coin - Salom rely	
	20		Sect. Cont. wagon,	
	21		bivouaced at the line by 10 on Back Coy	
	22		Coy Resting	
	23		Cleaning guns, etc.	
CANAL BANK	24		Chapel training upon Not Route march	
	25		Church Parade by Padre last march of the Fortress keeper with 15 Fusiliers etc	
	26		Coy Training	
	27		Coy Training including Burying Drills	
	28/29		Bivouac Drill, musketry lesson	
	30			
	31			

Signed / for Captain
Commanding 60th Machine Gun Company

15 Notts &
Derbys
Vol 2

www.ingramcontent.com/pod-product-compliance
Lightning Source LLC
Chambersburg PA
CBHW081243170426
43191CB00034B/2027